Complicated Compilation

Jessica Foster

Presentation by *BookLeaf Publishing*

Web: www.bookleafpub.com

E-mail: info@bookleafpub.com

ISBN: 9789358738247

First edition 2023

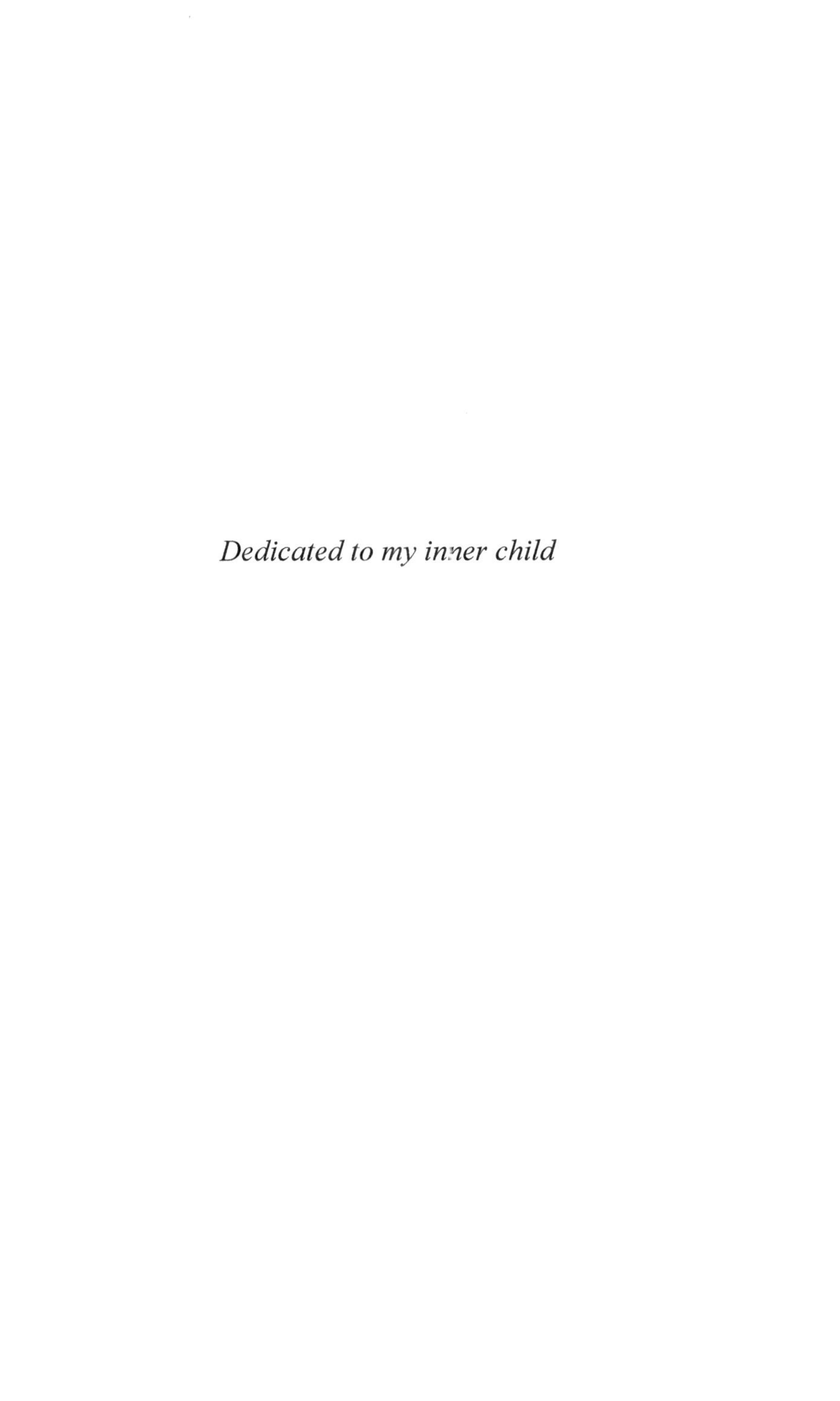

Dedicated to my inner child

ACKNOWLEDGEMENT

My gratitude goes out to all of the people who helped me along my journey, your care and support was instrumental to my existence. From the youngest age, until today, each and every one of you played a key role in my being the person that I am. Without your love, I wouldn't be here and neither would this book. Forever thankful for every instance of love, it all made a difference.

PREFACE

TRIGGER WARNING
The following poetical pieces include graphic
imagery pertaining to abuse.

Devotional Prayer 6.14.23

I'm not nice, but I can be very kind
Im not a doormat for you to wipe your feet on
I'm a magic carpet ride of the mind
I'm a lover, but a fighter in the right condition
Speaking on hurt isn't attention and commotion
It's about healing relationships broken
It's about feeling in a feeling-less ocean
It's about reeling from humans in motion
It's about stealing back your devotion
In my new reality I'm free as a finch
Tweeting to the world about the grift
That turned into the most beautiful gift
From the darkness of depression
To the light of lifting oppression
Comes back all of the love lost
Overflowing my cup at zero cost
Cheers to the people who break us
And mock our pain and suffering
Who tell us we are dramatic
When we are just buffering
As the soundtrack of life plays again
The eternal struggle to extract the darkness
Leaving me with a persistent question
Why can't I...
Just be grateful
Just be grateful for abuse

Just be grateful for inept parents
Just be grateful for friends who mock me
Just be grateful for family that drops me
Just be grateful for a soul rocked deep
It's hard to imagine anybody
Grateful for this dysfunctional shit
After all has been done and said
I'm grateful I don't know when to quit
I should be long gone by now
Sipping margaritas in the sky near the sun
Instead I stayed, worked and prayed
That our family wouldn't be done
I begged my brother to show up to moms funeral
I begged my other brother to carry
Some of the emotional weight
Of keeping this family on pace to recover
I begged my dad to invite everyone
To the one year ash spreading
When he said no, he guilted me abandonment
As if I hadn't had enough of it
My whole life time
Still I love with that decision
Knowing we hurt people and he doesn't care
When the five year came near
I invited everyone knowing it was the right thing
In the end it mattered nothing
Not included in the fourth family fun
Until the last minute like a bread crumb
To be grateful for, like a starving idiot, dumb

Hoping against all reason
He cares a little bit more than a heathen
And each time my heart breaks away
And that's on me for showing up
unconditionally
Since the first person molested me
Full of new knowledge
I dive head first into fixing this
Letting let a stranger on tiktok
Guide me to my past
He showed me what years of therapy lacked
How to save my inner child
We went back to ludington
To that apartment
Where the first hand touched me
Inappropriately
Before my favorite stuffed animal could be
Tainted by that silhouette of a man
Who reached into my crib
And cemented my first memory
A touch so disgusting
I scooped her up into my arms
Left everything behind
Waved goodbye to my mom
To my brothers
To the future abuse
Sexual, physical, verbal and other
I kept her safe
I held her hand, dried her tears

And honored her fears that were
Molded and shaped on Monroe Street
A house of horrors burnt to the ground
I told her over and over
We are safe now
With my eyes closed, my mind open
I visualized my little self
With curly brown pig tails
Dimples deep, and all the wind at her sails
Clutched in my arms as we moved far away
Around the bend, out of sight until we see
All the people waiting for me
The ones who love me unconditionally
Who won't hurt us like the people we leave
Who will welcome us, no need to debrief
We've finally made it out of darkness
And into a place where little jess can breathe
Tell her story in all it's gory
A safe space where she can write
About how she was so incredibly strong
In the face of so much wrong
She never lost that little light
That guided her intuitively away from the blight
Into the future, galloping at the speed of right
Where little Jess and big Jess, find it just might
Be ok to trust in the beauty of play
Stolen before she had enough words to say
This is my manifestation for children like me
That no matter our age, we can finally be free

Information Incoming
6.30.23

Information incoming…
Wait, hesitate, gravitate
Collaborate and listen
Jess is back with a brand new invention
Something, spirit grabs a hold of me tightly
Illuminates Illuminati like dark magic nightly
Nefarious femmes in a family line
Casting spells on a divine
Because their best can never outshine
No blood, and the family isn't all mine
Information incoming…
Wait, never mind
Soul family is coming online
No room at the inn for negative this time
Making space for my soul tribe ￼
See yourselves out, door is to the right
Laugh at the language of light
While you languish in liquor at night
Peace, be well, adios alright?
They warned you I was protected
And still you had to test it
And now we will see who is blessed
Times up, let's finally address it
Want my life, my fight but none of the strife

Want my creativity, bringability
But none of the drive
Want my wisdom, compassion
But none of the abuse to survive
Wants my vision, empathic system
But none of the light
I've been standing out since birth
I've been standing up since I knew my worth
I've been standing down since all this hurt
I've been standing in since the spiritual spurt
Information incoming…
Test results are in
Obstacles overcome
passed with intuition

It's me, Jess 7.4.23

Are you there, God?
It's me, Jess
I put in five years
While severely depressed
I begged brothers to stay
I included a father, I tried.
Are you hearing me, God?
I've been praying since mom died
I've been calling on spirits
To keep the family alive
I've made up events
Hoping for one single invite
From a dad who can't say sorry
Except to defend his right
To be as distant or aloof
While I'm left to fight
Emotions that tangle anger
And empathy because
He is not all-right
This is ducking exhausting
Do you feel me, God?
Is this that perplexing?
Or is he as cruel as he is odd?
My mind tries to explain to my heart
What my feelings can't dodge

What my healing can't pull apart
Are you scared of me, God?
He thinks I'm fragile like a bomb
Don't get too near, spare the rod
Too afraid I might talk about mom
Expressing dis-ease is a temper tantrum
Any raised voice is a violent nod
Call relatives, she's still upset
Pull up a chair, popcorn smell in the air
She's so explosive it's quite the spect
All it takes is a lil spark of unfair
She leaks gas like the hit was direct
Everyone's got blow torches aimed at her
Hoping to ignite an implosion of care
Do they think they know me, God?
Is it because I'm Kelly Greens Kid?
Is it due to unresolved trauma
That I used to flip a lid?
Is it due to narcissist family drama
That I can't hide or hid
The pain flowing like hot lava
Towards people who caused it
I finally sweet surrender
It's all that I have to give
To avoid a Sarah McLachlan bender
It's time to let go to live
Depart from them and allow my heart to tender

Real Remembers 7.6.23

In memory of Laurie "Raised By Wolves" Foster

Real talks, this life is hard
Real walks, this gait on guard
Real peeps, this truth be told
Real weeps, this hurt off hold
Real rocks, this roll is free
Real knocks, this toll is tea
Real keeps, this secret on lock
Real leaps, this fate off a rock
Real clocks, this expanse of time
Real blocks, this spell of rhyme
Real creeps, this dark of night
Real heaps, this flight or fight
Real heals, this pain in part
Real feels, this love of heart
Real flannels, this plaid of cover
Real channels, this language of lover
Real dopes, this breath an air
Real hopes, this depth of care
Real forgives, this family of that
Real gives, my mom a clap
Real amends, this fantasy from dream
Reals offends, this death was mean
Real exists, this fact is proven

Real persists, this trap in ruin
Real creates, this wand of magic
Real delineates, this mark of tragic
Real vanquishes, this thought of true
Real languishes, this memory is blue
Real remembers, this gift of life
Real remembers, this gift of strife
Real remembers

I can 7.19.23

I can because…
I can walk with the dark
Because I cast my own light
I can talk with the lark
Because I sing my own plight
I can run with the bulls
Because I free them to take flight
I can stun with the lulls
Because I dance to sources delight
I can feel with the strings
Because I love with all my might
I can heal with the reams
Because I tell with all I write
I can…

Burnt Bridges/Let It Go
7.20.23

Naw man I don't want to say it
I don't want replay it, or movie script it
Cast the cutest kids in it
Make all their stomachs turn
That fucking bridge must burn
Matches in their graspes
Ready to hand you your asses
When they find out why
Life made me want to die
A little bit inside
Every single day
That you chipped away
At the youngest of age
Making me always wonder
Why I'm not worthy of life
Why I'm so ducking sad
Why I can't be glad
Why I can't snap back
Why I can't talk smack
Flowers in the attic
Closely traumatic
My story is not automatic
It's in the radio static
And commonly tragic

Let it go, Jess
Let it go
Flower petals float
And it's time to denote
That despite my herstory
I'm still worthy
My ship has not sailed
My coffin not nailed
My strength yet unveiled
My talent no longer derailed
Let it go, yes
Let the truth go
Flower petals float
And they can't sink this boat
It's enroute to reach versions of me
Tossing temper tantrums
Unable to speak for their whole lives
Watch us all bleed in ink on the line
She's only 8, they will say
But one day she'll be assigned to read
A controversial poem written by me
Telling her story and maybe
She will pick a trusted person
And say "please read"
Catapulting in motion a rescuing commotion
Reaching to the bottom of hoping
Plucking her out of a future knowing
A cycle of abuse won't repeat while growing
A pattern created by others but hers beholding

Saving her year after year of self-loathing
Setting her on a path towards love overflowing
All because this controversial book
Is in her hands, won't let go holding
The answer is clear, speak up my dear
Keep speaking until you find the right ear
Hand them this book and tackle the truth
Tear by tear
That teacher that assigned this read
Is the best place to start

Plot Twist 7.21.23

Love is my lineage
If you go far enough back
Gratitude is my religion
If you exclude the times I was mad
Never ending practice
If you accept human traits
We error by design
We intentionally make mistakes
Alien is perfection
Master of emotions results in none
Apologetic is nature
Refusing is confusing to be blunt
All my life I channeled
This poetic voice to royal flush
Emotions unbecoming
In a house built on hush
Shared them with a teacher
Shoutout to Fergs
Learned how to put to paper
These emotions in words
Stolen from my bedroom
Threatened to tell the world
It's long past time to stop splashing around
To get serious about this gift I found
To travel and wander

To write everything down
To fulfill my destiny
To speak and make sound
Every time I think
It doesn't get better than this
Around the next corner
Is a new plot twist

The Test 7.23.23

Am I failing the test?
Thought I was doing my best
Thought I was taking the rest
Thought I was making a nest
Going back to high school
Repeat last year like a fool
Everyone moving on feels cruel
Chose to delay my own jewel
Can't get over the anger
Can't forgive the manger
Can't forget the danger
Can't admit I'm a stranger
Lost myself in the trauma
Lost my health in the drama
Lost my wealth in the karma
Lost my faith in my mama
All on me to make peace
All on me to desist or decease
All on me to decrease
All on me to release
The suffering
The wondering
The blundering
The thundering in my heart
That inches me apart

From anger to art
From disappointment to dart
Thrown at a map
Journey's repair systems zapped
Life's a mystery, let's leave it at that
Hurt people hurt people and that's a fact
And we're all guilty, all hands are filthy
All gardens unattended get wilt-y
All minds untethered get silty
Mines been weathered forever
Finally finding refuge in the sever
Taking true rest for the next endeavor
Bon voyage to never say never
Passing the test

Carole Baskin 7.23.24

Hey, thanks for askin'
Im not doing too great
Carole Baskin
I've made big decisions
Big emotions flowing
Write poems to release them
Usually privacy only me
Last one rushed to post
And looks like you all see
My wife's good
You can ask her
She tells me she's proud
She encouraged this tool
So I can heal after
Years of trying, crying
To the wrong people
If the flow is uncomfortable
My bad, but not really because
All I'm merely saying
Is that fixing trauma
That started when I was three
By a man raised by a mama
And hit again at 39
By an ending full of drama
That's a lot to process

And if I'm being honest
Its hard fucking work forgiving yourself
And others for their transgressions
Takes more than few years of therapy sessions
And don't get me started
On the elephant in the room
No, not doppelgängers daughter
Im talking about
When my mom became a ghost
Going through life's review
Bearing witness at most
To what happened in her purview
All the sexual abuse kept hidden
Physical, verbal she saw the tippy top
Broken baby me bed ridden
Pushing with all my strength
To get up
To get up
To get up
She finally saw it all
That's a lot to get over
Knowing she knows
Red rover, red rover!
Don't send me…
I want to stay alive!
This time around
I relied on telling
Family and friends
All about my suffering

Well, at least the dad stuff I did
Rather than boxing it up
Like I did when I was a kid
I tried to tell as much as I could
Without destroying reputations
But now I'm done
A couple years to process
Wasn't enough if you know
How far these wounds run
I try and try to move on
I see your eyes roll
At my lack of progress
That I think is quite complex
It breaks my heart less as
Im exiting depressed
And into acceptance
That shitty things happen
And shitty people get blessed
And hurt people get problems
And hurt people struggle to get dressed
Life is unfair
Don't worry about anyone
Except yourself
Lessons that sucks
Lack a human touch
But
After a few tough years
I get you think I'm lazy
I get you think I'm mad

I get you think I'm angry
Or I'm too much to be had
I won't keep you waiting because I know
People come and go for a reason
We are sometimes meant for a season
And some are exiled due to treason
Im not fighting anymore, I'm just leaving
But, really, is five years that long?
To deal with all that's gone wrong?
Or is it an investment only I'm banking on?
This is my life I'm saving
This is my life I'm recreating
This is my life I'm believing
This is my life I'm celebrating
Hey, thanks for askin'
I'm doing great!
Carole Baskin

Ope, I did it 7.24.23

Don't call it a comeback
I've been here for 44 years
I'm right on track
Writing wrong all of my fears
Transmuting generational trauma
With my pen tip
Typing all the drama
Finished with a click
Talking about childhood abuse hint hint
And all of the fallout that exists
Talking about neglect, abandonment
And the choices that persist
Hoping niece and nephews
Didn't experience the worst of this
Praying my voice eschews
The silent suffering twist
The cycle ended in my line
No adult children who unalive
At some point in their life
Unable to cope with what wasn't right
Abusers don't have to do
A single thing to fix
The souls they broke in two
They just have to convince
Everyone the squeaky wheel

Is probably off her meds
I'm steady on my dose
I'm flushing what you did from my head
Making waves for the table
High tide lifts all boats
Saving face for generations unable
To speak up and emote
What abuse unchecked
Can often lead to
More kids wrecked
By no one knowing what to do
Ask and really listen
And by all means believe
I was only seven
When my mom trusted him, instead of me
That lead to years of torture
Knowing my words were hot air
What terrible things culture
In environments with adults who don't care
To do difficult things
To talk about tough stuff
To admit they are human beings
Who error and fuck up
Instead of helping the hurting
They rather double up the pain
Ensuring it continues
Instead of taking blame
To my niece and nephews
I apologize for being silent all these years

For hiding in plain sight
Because I was swallowed up by fear
It was then and still is hard to say
And that quiet created an opportunity
For the same sad story to play
I'm so very sorry
There was more I could do
No excuses, all apology
Chance after chance I blew
But truth be known
I buried deep this thorn and thistle
So I could get grown
Then one day reality
Sprung like a spring from the box
And took up residence quickly
And forced me to beat the clock
Before this shame consumes
And couples with parental abandonment
I want to release volumes
Of herstory to change repeat entanglement
They say it's never too late
So here I am to say my truth
So this hideous fate
Escapes the next Foster youth

Pause 7.25.23

Pause
Take a moment and reflect
My self worth has taken a lifetime hit
And yet I kept rising out of all of it
Be Proud
Look around at what you built while on fire
An empire built out of chicken wire
A respite my weary heart desired
Love
The fault in me is loving them all
Intuition hitting ignore for the call
The writing was always on the wall
Accept
This little light of mine
I'm going to keep letting it shine
I'm going to heal in rhyme

Don't Believe Enough?
7.26.23

Around five years old
I went to Sunday school
The snacks were cool
Around seven years of age
I went to a baptist one in east lake
All work no play except a Halloween thing
Questioning everything is fun
Not for the teachers having none
You just have to believe in the son
But where'd he go those years missing
I bet the stories are interesting
Threatened with hell for not listening
I asked my mom if I had to go
Never went back to religion…so..
I still had questions I must know
Why did that man do that to me at three?
Why did the boy at seven force my mouth on his
pee-pee?
Why at eight did my best boy friend
Place my hand on his nether region
Why did I return home and tell the brother guilty
of treason
Who a year earlier when I told my mom
About truth or dare and being forced upon

It was too late at eight to exercise good
judgement
Upon telling my brother why my friend had
done
He pulled me into the bathroom
For a personal demonstration
And they was the beginning of the end

Why did god abandon me?
Is he teaching me a lesson on belief?
Is he mad at me for questioning?
Because I don't understand anything!
I'm getting mad at everything!
I can't stand this is all so maddening!

Age nine, another boy, another violate
WWE wrestling, I go into the bedroom
To retrieve a toy, turn around, pushed back
On a bed, fully clothed, I thank whatever
Is listening to my heart cry out loud
What my words won't come out
His body weight presses and gyrates
He finishes, I lay obliterated
Before I can move, it's his 18 yo
Cousins turn
I don't thank anything this time
I just cry, but not until I escape the house
Find my bedroom, hide inside
Age ten, perfect age to consent

Along comes sex education
And the sudden realization
That I know how to escape them
My bedroom became
The only place
Where no one could touch me
No one could make me touch them
No one could break the lock
No one could pierce the fort
No one could make me go back
No one could hurt me for sport
It also became
The place where
I wrote my first stories
I wrote hundreds of poems
I painted Janis Joplin
I sang off key
As Ani DiFranco rescued me
I want to be
A Joyful Girl
I want to be happy
I want to play in the light
I want to be care free
I don't want to fear
I don't want to lash out
I want so badly out of here
Because of all I keep inside
Stuff I can't let out
I want to smile more

I want to cry less
I want to live a long life
But all this makes me stressed
Just hang on, my inner child cries
It's not that long, she promises every night
Just hang on, my inner teen screams
Graduation and exploration, our dreams
The high of holding the Willy Wonka winner
Falls apart with a one way ticket dim glimmer
I seem ungrateful but what they don't know
It was my only escape plan
Seattle was going to be my saving grace
Now my exit is delayed
Cry it all out
I apologized profusely
I thanked them both for the gift
I was determined
To make the most of the trip
Instead I came back knowing
A lesbian couldn't live
With an affluent (read conservative) Aunt
And rain that was never slowing
Back to the drawing board
Depression inches back in
Apply to colleges, pray for scholarships
Work 40 hours at the grocery store
Volunteer to coach volleyball
These girls think I'm the oddest ball
But in the dark of winter is when I fall apart

And I needed anything at all
Dinners with coworkers
Anything to not be home
Finally I'm accepted to gay valley
There's a light at the end of a tunnel called hope
Just hang on, it's so close it's hard to believe
All of me is gripping tight to the dream
The day came, I went away
Placed a rainbow flag on my desk
Roommate hugged me, told the whole floor
Mad at first, violations still hurt
But surrendering to her good work
It was clear, there was something
High above after all
As a tribe called 4th Floor Kistler Girls
Took me in and let some of my armor fall
Everything in the past
Disappeared like a bad dream
I had so much to look forward to
I could finally be me
And all these girls had no idea
What still lie beneath
But they made space for me to believe
That everything happens for a reason
That there's more to the universe
Than just planets and star dust
This was exactly where I was meant to be
Even if just for a season
So I could learn what it's like to be free

I never found God in church
But easily saw something greater than us
In all that I could see
Even the people who broke me
I always wondered who broke them first
If God placed a curse
If they were wielded a much bigger hurt
And in the end telling my truth
Feels like piling on more dirt
But the fact of the matter
Is we all have worth
And no God with all the powers
Would bless athletes, but children he deserts
No, it never worked like that
The spirit, the source, the power
It's all a choice and that's why
Three year olds can't stop
What twelve year old me learned to do
God works through all people
There's a god in me
And the people who hurt me too
And collectively let's weep
For what we and god do and don't do

Gracie Lou FreeBush 7.27.23

Grace, the courteous goodwill kind
Is also a blessing before dinner time
It's a song about god saving thee
And it's the name of Miss Congeniality
It's a gift of a blessing
It's a bit distressing
When your inner teen wants to scream
But your higher self dares to dream
That destroying the cage sets all of us free
Unconditional love isn't just a myth
I'm starting to really see
It's the foundation of all of this
Grace isn't just amazing
Or a pledge to play ball
It's the hearts way of grazing
On love which conquers all
Anger is valid against injustice
And boundaries must be clear
Distance necessary for respite
Grace to empathize a sign of love not fear
There but before the grace of god go I
Here but for the grace of us go we
Humility a must not just for audience
But privately so no need for correcting
The opposite of shut up and sit down

Is grace for the unintentional inflicting
The emotional iq to tell the truth
Isn't war that will never cease
Gracie Lou FreeBush said it best
"I really do want world peace"

Search Party 7.27.23

Music is just poetry
With a melodic accompaniment
Poetry is just music
Without accoutrements
Life is just existing
Without enjoyment
Existing is just life
So make the most of it
Leave the past behind
And the people unkind
Prepare for the future
It's finally arrived
Try not to forget
the human experiment
Try not to get lost
By all the detriment
For once, no twice you were lost
Twice now you've returned to fun
The hardest lesson to remember
We are all a search party of one

Scars Into Stars 7.28.23

Turning scars into stars
Isn't overnight work
It's a lifelong process
To alchemize the hurt
Transmute the energy
From people not understanding
Why you can't fake life
Pretend like everything's alright
Deny the suffering and plight
Of yourself until the night
Selfish stories dim your light
Making it harder to craft
Scars into stars
Just choose the life raft
Of denial check emotion
Feelings aren't fact
It's all in your head
Gas lighter highlighter
Why this work they dread
Chiron Wounded Warrior
Leave the swords in the past
Medicinal woman's salve
Turns broken into healed fast
Bag balm tissue torn
Open air heals at last

Speaking on the topic
Truth really sets you free
To turn your scars into stars
For the whole world to see

Truth Hurts 7.31.23

The truth hurts
That's why I kept it to myself
The words I speak
People ignore what's dealt
Ignorance is bliss
When the truth makes you squirm
Process the diss
Integrity loose like a worm
Facts are thin
Asking questions gets answers
Logic can win
Tip toe around reality like dancers
Come to a conclusion
Without any information
Don't want to believe
So we'll just support the thief
My truth was settled
When I was a teen
If you don't want the world to know
You shouldn't do bad things
That's not a threat to go
Nor a blackmail with wings
That's merely a fact
I've always been a truth seeker
An unfortunate matter speaker

Shame will keep some things on lock
Until it's going to take you down with her
Breaking chains to set you free
Is the only option around
For a person as bold as I
It's a shock how I've kept mum
But I loved my family
More than I loved my freedom
Once I decided I don't want a family
Built on sweet little white lies
Let that foundation crumble
And let liars scramble to hide
I've unhitched my wagon
From a dysfunctional pact
Of people pretending things are fine
While drinking a 4th drink wine
After shooting shots before dinner time
Musing over the crazy one
Calling out all of her dysfunction
While Harry's rolling in his grave
Embarrassed of his kin and how the behave
Treating whistleblowers
Like terrorists infiltrating from within
In a world full of "good people"
With a habit of doing bad things
Unapologetic and arrogantly taking swings
One sentence dedicated to
A single misunderstanding
The rest ranting Shut Up and Sit Down

With family falling in line
So brave! Bravo!
Put her in her place!!!!
How dare she talk about her life
How dare she correct us in plain sight
I don't need anyone to believe me
The truth is the truth
And what's done in the dark
Will always come to light
So wiggle and try to fight
But in the end the good lord knows
My words burn for a reason
My words sting those caught cheating
Truth hurts best be believing
In unhealthy love, we will all be bleeding

Psycho Analyze 8.1.23

Psycho analyze my methods
Trauma dump vs therapy poetry
Exposed vs truths unloaded
Airing dirty laundry vs telling my story
Perspective is subjective
Minimal facts collected
No lies in this poem detected
Black sheep easily rejected
It's alright I always say
For nearly four decades
What else can one say
When justice always escapes?
Nobody should keep quiet that long
But support was always gone
Speaking up deemed as wrong
Feelings about the facts sad song
If healing cptsd were so easy
If dealing with narcissists
In a family that insists
On telling me to sit down
Shut up and barely exist
Was breezy
I'd have been healed by now
To which I generally hear
From family with a caring ear

You don't understand
Blah blah blah
But it's not me who lacks command
On the big picture
And the collateral damage
Generations addicted
Vodka, Beer, Gin
Weed, Food, you name it
None of us escaped it
And it's not just blood line
Adopted family
Has its own history
Of turning kitchen counters
Into elaborate bars
By the end of the night
Empty bottles
Of wine, gin and lemon cello
Permeate the space
What do the kids think?
What message was received?
Handle life with a drink
Or ten
That struggle to heal
From generations
Of dysfunction
Keeping it classy
Pinky finger in the air
Everybody declare
The problem isn't here

How dare she say otherwise
That things are less than fine
That things aren't sublime
In a family foundation
Rotting in lies
Taking sides
When I asked that
We all take it in stride
Give him time
To understand
How brutal their choice
Had to land
Fist hitting a house of cards
Tell a simple truth
It all falls apart
Instead let him believe
Cutting your kids out
Is nothing to apologize for
Get over it they implore
Story of my life
Be Brave or stupid
You decide
Whichever the case
I feel obliged
To make clear
That this time
I will not back down
From truths told
In rhyme or riddle

In text or calls
In therapy sessions
Years ago
I won't then
Nor I ever will
Apologize for what
I've been through
If my words cut deep
Try for a fucking second
To Imagine 8 year old me
Messages sent
Messages received
Easiest to neglect
Easier to deflect
Easier to protect
Than know what God knows
To do what God wants
To make tough choices
You think kid me
Should have done
Adult me struggled to go
And now I'm cracked
Starting to hatch
Turn that hurt into Art
Tell the world
How I fell apart
Only to put myself back together
Making art imitate life from the start

Hiding Mind 8.2.23

Twenty twenty three
Something broke inside me
No more bullshit
No more saying sorry
For speaking truth
For unleashing facts
For bringing to light
What was done in the dark
To no longer be confined
By people
Who are only sorry
The got caught
Thru trauma, nightmares
Suicidal thoughts
I fought to be here
So I won't take
the truth back
I'll keep telling
Dirty details
Until the weight I carry
Drops to zero
This was never
My burden to bear
This was always
My hurt to declare

Justice isn't fair
In the arena
Of opinion
And people who
Weren't there
My freedom
Is a dream won
God knows
This must be done
Foundations crumble
Built on secrets
Rotting the pillars
Holding up the place
Foundations rebuilt
On the truth
Support pillars
Holding the roof
A house that can last
Sturdy on land
Structure beneath
Solid and grand
Forged in fire
To tear down
What couldn't last
To create on ground
A life less stressed
Forever grateful
For this ability
To let go of the hateful

Sides have been taken
To uphold a reputation
Enable unstable foundation
Throw away the foresaken
My faith has gifted me
The ability to see
The bigger picture
And that's why I believe
Everything happens
For a reason
And it's all in
Universes timing
Without inspired action
We can't get traction
By addition and subtraction
Watch flow fraction
Let go now
Sit back relax
And watch the past
Implode and collapse
Birthing a rebuild
Greater than
the dilapidated
Mental space
That dominated
the landscape
A cage created
To keep sane
To uphold an image

To hide family stains
Dirty laundry
Doesn't go
On the
Outside line
It dries in
The basement
It takes more time
That's why
I'm no longer hiding mine
Or hiding mind

Anchors aweigh 8.2.23

The truth sets you free
Anchors aweigh
Cycles complete
Can't overstay
Lessons learned
Characters revealed
Sentiments are sweet
But can't derail
A departure overdue
From unfriendly confines
Refuse to shut up and sit down
Stay standing this time
No time to waste bitching
About who's fault
No time to waste asking
What else is in the vault
Want details without contrition
You must be kidding
Read it and weep
In the NYT best seller edition
Five years was plenty
To recognize humility
All the worlds opportunity
To admit the futility
Of denying the truth

That endings like that
Hurt more than one
Can get over with tit for tat
Stretched over time
And distance I won't forget this
There's a message
To share for others stuck in this
Unable to get dressed
Trapped in their head
Feeling unworthy
Followed by existential dread
What happened to you
Wasn't your fault
What happens for you
Is to catapult
Into the next chapter
Where life can begin
Devoid of bad actors
Making room for new kin
If you're struggling
To know what I mean
Imagine a person
You need to stop juggling
Picture the people
Who only take up space
In your head and your heart
You never see their face
There's no reciprocate
There's no calls or text

There's no effort to fix
Issues that are complex
These aren't your people
It's hard to admit
They're someone else's
With you there's no commit
Ah! Do you see?
Letting go, who do you dread?
The person
Who popped in your head
That's the one
To let go with no regret
And once you accept
It's ok to grieve
Yes, it is sad indeed
When family has to leave
People you can't retrieve
Thought you couldn't live without
But yet, you're not deceased
An EX of any kind
Isn't worth waiting for
When you could grow
And discover all that's in store
It's painful
Trust me I know
But time passes anyway
Why not choose to glow?
We all say we want it
But our minds hit replay

Actively choosing
That these people won't go away
Now is the time to change
So don't think about waste
Time is always right
To do what is best
Call it what you want
But it's basically a test
All you have to do is choose
Love over depressing
If a lesson can be learned
Is love for self
Not the best blessing earned!
Perspective is subjective
But most do not regret
Walking away from the past
Into future's vignette

Strange Beauty 8.12.23

There's a strange beauty
In letting your old life die
Watching the flames
Transform and lick the sky
Ushering you a safe distance
Away to gaze upon the display
Yellow tape barricades
Mornings sun exposes charred remains
Wherever I'm going
I can't go back to unsafe
There's a strange beauty
In knowing I'm on my way
Grounded in growing
Unlimited chances to get going
This is the greatest unfolding
Once I trust in the process of molding
Moments making me
Instead of the other way around
Dreams steeped in magical belief
Instead of logic and financial bound
When in rome and in doubt
No need to follow the locality
Instead, follow your heart to where
There's a strange beauty

Rock Bottom 8.18.23

Rock bottom, is a good place to be
Take a break, rest, and just breathe
Lost it all in the fall, having nothing
Is freeing, to know you've got something
Inside of you, capable of beginning
Over again, from here every step is winning
Rock bottom, it's not meant to be
Comfortable, but it should be safely
Situated, where life can be recreated
Allowing, new plans to be deviated
Away, from the past, alleviated
Face the future, resume abbreviated
To include, self-help guru
For taking care of myself
When there was no one left to